MYTHOLOGY UNLEASHED
Timeless Tales from our Glorious Past

Foreword by
Revathy Sankaran

Divya Balasundaram

Illustrated by: Vidya Balasundaram

DEDICATION

We humbly dedicate this book to

Our Amma – B. Karpagam

&

Our Appa – V. Balasundaram

Divya & Vidya

CONTENTS

FOREWORD

It is with great joy and pride that I introduce this remarkable collection of Indian mythological stories. These sacred tales, passed down through generations, form the very soul of Indian culture and spirituality. They are not just stories—they are the living essence of a tradition that celebrates the divine in the world around us and within ourselves. Through the lives of Gods, Goddesses, and great epic heroes, we are reminded of universal truths: the triumph of good over evil, the power of devotion, and the eternal quest for righteousness.

As you turn these pages, may you be drawn into the rich tapestry of India's spiritual heritage and find meaning that resonates with your own journey. These stories, as they have always done, carry the power to illuminate and transform, offering not only lessons of the past but also guidance for the present and future.

I invite you to immerse yourself in these divine tales and to experience the awe and inspiration they bring, as they continue to light the path for seekers of truth.

On a personal note, I have known the family for a long time, and Divya-Vidya sisters are well-versed in various art forms.

Divya's quest and thirst for knowledge must have prompted her to pen down this collection of gems for posterity. This book will be very useful for young mothers to narrate stories to their children.

With best wishes and blessings,

'Kalaimamani' Smt. Revathy Sankaran,
Former Editor of Mangayar Malar,
Storyteller, TV Anchor, Actor.

ENDORSEMENT

"*Mythology Unleashed* masterfully illuminates the ancient tapestry of Indian mythology, weaving together divine narratives with profound cultural wisdom. The author's vivid storytelling brings to life legendary figures - from the sagacious Vidura and Drona to Lord Vishnu's cosmic avatars - while making complex spiritual concepts accessible to readers of all ages. Through insightful tales that explore both the grandeur and compassion of divine beings, this remarkable collection serves as more than just stories; it's a spiritual journey into India's rich heritage. Each page reveals timeless moral lessons and profound wisdom, making it an essential read for anyone drawn to the mystical realms of ancient lore. I congratulate Divya and wish her a grand success as an author."

– Dr. Subhash Sharma,

Best Selling Author, Keynote Speaker, Most Admired Global Indian Awardee, Ivy League Alumnus, Mentor of Change(NITI Aayog-India), Business Coach of the Year Awardee, Veteran Sea Warrior, Youth Mentor, Founder of SKS Universe, and Humanitarian

ACKNOWLEDGEMENTS

First and foremost, I would like to acknowledge the role of my mother and father in initiating me into this beautiful world of our culture and tradition. Through literature and various art forms like dance and music, any opportunity to kindle our interests about our culture has never been missed. Words cannot do justice to the efforts taken by my mother to instil tradition and values as an integral part of our life, and the more difficult part, retain it in us even as we grew. Our capabilities are purely driven by the steep determination and resolve of our parents to not settle for anything less than perfect for their children. My grandparents deserve a special mention here, who have passed on a lot of their values to us through value-based storytelling and spiritual services. This book is a reflection of my roots – my grandparents and parents.

I would like to acknowledge the efforts of my father at this moment – what started as a simple blog and a Facebook page, took shape as a book purely due to his vision and humongous efforts. He has walked the last mile in ensuring every detail of this book is perfect, just as he is! I would also like to thank my sister, Vidya, who has taken utmost responsibility to make sure this book is flawless and in shape. From being a critical reviewer (and a very strict one too!) to bringing the book alive with her wonderful illustrations, she has been a constant companion in this journey. This book is a product of their hard work.

I would like to thank my husband – Vignesh – for being a pillar of support in bringing out this piece of work. His constant push on me to do more is something that keeps me motivated. My two lovely children, Shravya & Shreyas, deserve a special mention too! I would also like to thank my mother-in-law and father-in-law for always encouraging me to pursue my interests with no boundaries. Without my family's support, this book wouldn't be.

PREFACE

With the rich landscape of culture that India has to offer, this book tries to present to its readers some significant experiences from tales and characters that will impart lessons and values to the forthcoming generations. Each of these stories offers a deeper understanding of the complexities of life, the absence of just black and white, the nature of good and evil, and the significance of Dharma.

The stories have been drawn from various religious texts such as the epics, puranas, and even regional tales from the past. Bharat is such a vast country that even the great epic Ramayana is not bound by Valmiki's sole narration. We have different versions or retellings of the epic, such as Kambaramayanam and Ramcharitmanas. Also, there are numerous stories all over the country based on different versions of Ramayana. Similar is the case with Mahabharata, puranas, and regional tales. All these versions may not be fully consistent with each other. Within these constraints, this book tries to present stories that would be interesting as well as informative to the readers.

The objective of this book would be met if these stories inspire today's young kids, reminding them that the themes of love, duty, courage, and sacrifice are timeless and universal. I hope this knowledge from the past guides our present and future.

Welcome to a realm where the divine and the earthly intertwine, and where every story has the power to transform!

BIRTH OF LORD GANESHA

Every ritual in our culture is begun by invoking Lord Ganesha. Vinayaka, Vigneshwara, Pillayar, and Ganapathy, as he is fondly called by his devotees, is known to bestow success on his worshippers. The following story narrates the birth of Lord Ganesha and why he became the Elephant-headed God!

Lord Shiva, one of the Supreme Gods in Hindu culture, was married to Goddess Parvathi (also known as Shakthi), and together they spent their days in Kailash, their abode in the Himalayan mountains.

One day, Goddess Parvathi called upon Nandi, the loyal follower of Lord Shiva, to guard their gate while she went in to bathe. Within a few minutes, Lord Shiva walked in front of the gates, and Nandi was caught in a dilemma. As per Goddess Parvathi's order, he had to stop Lord Shiva at the gate, but he was a strong loyalist of the Lord, and who could think of barring the Lord from entering his own house? Thus wondering, Nandi let Lord Shiva pass the gate.

The Young Lad

On seeing Lord Shiva, Goddess Parvathi was infuriated that Nandi had disregarded her commands. After hours of thought, she realised that unless she had a loyalist of her own, there would be no soul who would respect her the way the Lord's followers respected him. She decided to create her own loyalist and sculpted an idol using a paste from her body. She imparted life to the statue, and right in front of her stood a handsome young lad, all decked in energy and valour. Goddess Parvathi was jubilant about her creation and blessed him with unique powers and strengths.

A few days later, she asked him to guard her gate as she had asked Nandi to do earlier. Just as before, Lord Shiva tried to walk past the gate but he was stopped by the young lad. Lord Shiva was enraged at the idea that a random boy was preventing his entry into his own place. The boy simply waved his staff at Lord Shiva and would not move despite any amount of cajoling that it was his own place.

Lord Shiva left the place fuming at the thought that he was sent out from his own abode. He sent a horde of men to fight the young lad who had insulted him. The army of soldiers, led by Nandi, known for his courage and strength, reached the place only to be defeated by the young lad in a jiffy. They hurried back to Lord Shiva and narrated the happenings. Lord Shiva felt insulted at the thought that his army had to suffer a defeat at the hands of a lone, young boy. He led the warpath to the place where the young lad stood guarding the gate, as cheerful as ever.

The ensuing war between Lord Shiva and the young lad was fearful. Slowly, the Lord began to realise that the lad did possess extraordinary strengths and skills. Unable to quell his wrath, he aimed his all-conquering Trishul at the young boy. The Trishul found its mark and slew the head of the young lad.

Hearing the commotion, Goddess Parvathi ran out, only to find her beloved creation lying on the ground, lifeless. She cried her heart out and declared that her son had to be brought back to life and must obtain an honourable position.

Elephant-headed God

Lord Shiva was now filled with remorse over his actions. He agreed to bring him back to life and ordered his men to go in search of a replacement for the young lad's head. He instructed them to slay and bring to him the head of the first creature that they came across in the northern direction. The men set out in the northern direction and finally came upon an elephant. They slew the head of the elephant and brought it back to Lord Shiva. Lord Shiva then affixed the head of the elephant to the young lad's body and brought him back to life.

The young lad was none other than Lord Ganesha, brought back to life with an elephant head. Lord Shiva blessed him and accepted him as his son. He announced that henceforth, Lord Ganesha would be worshipped at the beginning of all endeavours, as a remover of obstacles, as a destroyer of evils, and as the God of Wisdom, Knowledge and Wealth.

Vinayaka Sloka:

*Shuklam Baradharam Vishnum, Shashi Varnam Chatur
Bhujam
Prasanna Vadanam Dhyayet Sarva Vighnopashantaye*

Meaning:

Praise be to the Lord who is wearing white clothes, who is all-pervading, who is as bright as the moon and has four hands, who has a compassionate face. Let us meditate on him to ward off all obstacles.

...

Matsya Avatar – The First of the Ten

Matsya Avatar was the first incarnation of Lord Vishnu, taking the form of a fish ('Matsya' in Sanskrit).

The Need Arises

Once, after a tiresome day of his creation duties, Lord Brahma retired to sleep.

As soon as he fell asleep, a demon named Hayagriva, who had an eye on the Vedas, emerged and eloped with the four Vedas. He hid himself under the deep oceans, assuming that no one would be able to find him there. Lord Vishnu, the Protector of all, had noticed this and decided to protect the Vedas. He had to assume the responsibility of saving the Vedas from the treacherous demon.

Also, at the end of that Yuga, all the three worlds were going to be submerged in the ocean. Lord Vishnu decided that he would also preserve one species from each flora and fauna so that they could flourish in the next Yuga.

He decided to take the form of a fish to achieve these two purposes: save the Vedas from the demon and preserve species for the next Yuga.

The Matsya Avatar

King Manu, who was an ardent devotee of Lord Vishnu, was chosen by the Lord to carry out this mission. The Lord appeared in the form of a fish and gave the king the necessary instructions. He told the king that the three worlds would submerge in the ocean in exactly seven days and that Manu had to accommodate animals, plants and seeds of various types in a ship dispatched by the Lord Himself. Also to be saved were the Saptarishis (or the Seven Sages). The Lord advised the king to carry along with him Vasuki, the Serpent king, as he would be of some help in the mission. Lord Vishnu, in the form of Matsya, also told the king that he would meet him at the required time and left the king to perform his duties.

On the other hand, the Lord had to vanquish the demon, Hayagriva, and restore the Vedas to Lord Brahma. He assumed the form of a huge fish, a form that would not even fit in rivers, and killed the demon. The Lord restored the Vedas to Lord Brahma once he woke up after the end of the Pralaya.

Having fulfilled his first mission, the Lord set out to find King Manu, who had completed the instructions given by the Lord. He had assembled all the species, the Saptarishis and Vasuki on board and was awaiting the arrival of the Lord. The devastating rains had already begun, and the entourage was sincerely hoping that their Lord would save them from the destruction.

Lord Vishnu, in the form of Matsya, advised King Manu to tie the ship to his horn using the Serpent king, Vasuki. Once this was done, the fish escorted them to safety amidst a growling ocean and harsh weather. He held onto them protectively until the rains and floods receded.

Lord Vishnu then imparted the highest knowledge of Brahman to Manu and the seven sages.

Matsya Sloka:

Nirmagna sruthi jaala maargana dasaa dathakshanair veekshanai:
Antha thanvadhiva aravinda gahanaan oudanvatheenaam apaam.
Nishprathyooha tharanga ringana mitha: prathyooda paatha: chadaa.
Dola Aaroha sadohalam bhagavatha: maatsyam vapu: paathu na:

Meaning: The Lord dived into the ocean in the form of a fish, searched with His lotus eyes, rapidly viewing in all directions, creating an illusion of lotus flowers blossoming everywhere - all in search of the Vedas that had been stolen by an Asura. The ebb and flow of the waves of the Ocean seemed to be a swinging cradle that soothed and almost lulled Him into a comfortable reverie. May this Lord of the 'Matsya Avatar' protect us.

SATYAVATI – THE MAJESTIC QUEEN

Satyavati, the character from Mahabharata, epitomises courage and confidence. Her determination to retain the Bharata Empire with the Kurus (a clan which lived during the Vedic period) drove her to extremely tough situations, and she sailed through them with her decisive style of management, along with her stepson, the venerable Bhishma.

Birth & Early Days of Satyavati

Satyavati was born to the Chedi King, Vasu, and Adrika, a cursed Apsara-turned fish. Since she was born of a fish, she was also known as Matsyagandha (one with the odour of a fish). She was also known as Yojanagandha (one with a fragrance that extended to a yojana - 7 to 8 miles) and Kali (the dark one). Satyavati was then adopted by the chief of the fishermen in the kingdom and was lovingly brought up. She assisted her father in ferrying people across the river Yamuna.

A Divine Child

On one such instance, Satyavati offered to ferry Sage Parashara across the river. The sage found her beautiful and longed for a relationship with Satyavati. After requesting for a boon to protect her reputation and everlasting fame for the child who would be born from their relationship, Satyavati accepted his proposal.

On the same day, she gave birth to the divine child, named Krishna (not to be confused with Lord Krishna, the Avatar of Lord Vishnu). The child grew up to become one of the most revered sages of all times and came to be known as Sage Vyasa. He also drew fame as he went on later to write the epic, Mahabharata.

Marriage with Shantanu

Satyavati grew up to be an embodiment of beauty and fragrance. One day, King Shantanu, who ruled over Hastinapura, happened to see her and wanted to marry her. When he put forth his proposal to her, Satyavati coyly accepted and requested him to speak to her father. Shantanu agreed and reached out to her father, who was willing to give her hand in marriage on the fulfilment of a condition. He asked Shantanu to promise that only the son born to Satyavati would be eligible to rule the kingdom and not Devavrata, who was the elder son of Shantanu (Devavrata was born to Shantanu and Ganga, who was his first wife).

Shantanu refused to promise this and returned to his palace grief-stricken, as he could not bring himself to surrender his dear son's rights for his pleasure. Over the next few days, he lost interest in other affairs and was haunted by thoughts of

Satyavati day and night. Devavrata, on observing his father's sick state, found out the real reason behind his illness and visited the chief of fishermen seeking the hand of Satyavati for his father. On hearing the condition imposed, Devavrata took an oath that he would never in his life demand rights on the kingdom. The chief was still not satisfied, and Devavrata went a step ahead to take the vow of celibacy. From then on, he was called Bhishma.

Satyavati's father now agreed; Bhishma returned to the palace with Satyavati and got her married to Shantanu. Shantanu and Satyavati begot two sons, Chitrangada and Vichitraveerya. After Shantanu passed away, Bhishma installed Chitrangada on the throne under the command of Satyavati.

Loss of Sons – A Forlorn Mother

But as luck would have it, Chitrangada died in a battle with another king. When Vichitraveerya came of age, Bhishma tried to get him married. He arranged for Vichitraveerya's marriage with Ambika and Ambalika, the princesses of Kasi.

Vichitraveerya lost his life a few years after his marriage, and Satyavati's fear came true. The kingdom now did not have any heir. Satyavati requested Bhishma to ascend the throne and rule the kingdom. She also suggested that he get married so that the line of Shantanu would continue. Bhishma, however, replied that he could never renounce his word. He could hence never ascend the throne nor get married, as per his vow.

In ancient times, there existed a tradition called 'Niyoga', where a man could be called upon to help a woman bear children to extend the family's progeny. This entailed following a few rules to avoid misuse. The people involved had to keep in mind that they were implementing Niyoga only for Dharma and not for pleasure. Niyoga was practiced only with revered men, again to avoid the element of misuse. The rules also made it clear that the man who fathered the child could not claim any rights over the child.

Bearing in mind this tradition, Satyavati called upon her son, Sage Vyasa, to ensure that Hastinapura would have heirs. When Ambika saw the rugged looks of the sage, she closed her eyes and hence her son, Dhritarashtra, was born blind. The second queen, Ambalika, grew pale on seeing his frightful appearance and hence her son, Pandu, was born with a pale complexion. On the third instance, Ambika, reminded of his fearsome face, sent her maid in her place. The child she gave birth to, Vidura (incarnation of Lord Dharma), was blessed to be a very intelligent and virtuous man.

Later Life

Dhritarashtra married Princess Gandhari (the princess from Gandhara), and Pandu married Princess Kunti (the adopted daughter of Kuntibhoja, also known as Pritha) and Princess Madri (the princess of Madra). Gandhari performed certain religious rites and gave birth to 100 sons who later came to be known as the Kaurava princes. Kunti & Madri gave birth to five sons with the help of a mantra which Sage Durvasa had taught Kunti during her early days. These children grew up to be known as the Pandava princes.

Satyavati was tormented by the problem of a lack of heir to her kingdom. The death of Shantanu when her sons were barely a few years old and the deaths of her sons at very early ages left the throne of Hastinapura in question many times. Why did such situations keep arising repeatedly in Satyavati's life?

According to Hindu belief, the effect of Karma leaves none unaffected. That which is done to others would return to the doer. In Satyavati's life, it was her father who nullified Bhishma's progeny. An entire descendant race was wiped out due to his oath of celibacy. This curse of Karma followed Satyavati for generations and kept the throne of Hastinapura worried.

The fight between these cousins triggered the famous Kurukshetra war in the Mahabharata. Foreseeing the events that would cause misery to the family, Sage Vyasa advised Satyavati to retire from her worldly life to the forest. Satyavati, along with her two queens, Ambika and Ambalika, retired to the forest where, after a few years of penance, she died.

Thus ended the saga of an obedient daughter, a dutiful wife, a caring mother, and a decisive queen.

THE STORY OF SHAKTHI & SHIVA

Lord Shiva, one of the three Supreme Lords of the world (the other two Lords being Lord Vishnu and Lord Brahma), is known for his powers of destruction of evil forces, his benevolence, his anger, the Third Eye, and the dance form attributed to him – Thaandava. Goddess Shakthi, on the other hand, is known to be a personification of strength, valour and courage.

Sati weds Shiva

Goddess Shakthi, the consort of Lord Shiva, was born to King Daksha (son of Lord Brahma) and was named Sati. Even as a child, she was a staunch devotee of Lord Shiva. When the appropriate time drew closer, Daksha decided to get her married. On consulting Sati, he understood that she would marry none other than Lord Shiva himself. She announced that she would perform severe penances and win the hand of Lord Shiva.

Sati engaged herself in meditation and prayed to Lord Shiva. Awestruck by her powerful penance, Lord Shiva appeared in front of her and asked her what boon she would want. She requested him to take her as his consort, and Lord Shiva agreed (as he already knew Sati was an incarnation of

Goddess Shakthi). He approached Daksha and sought his daughter's hand for marriage. After gaining his acceptance, Sati & Shiva married. They happily resided in the Himalayas, the abode of Lord Shiva.

Once, Lord Shiva, accompanied by Sati, attended a Yagna (spiritual pyre) organised by Rishis. The yagna was attended by the Devas and other celestials. Daksha was also an invitee to the yagna. When he entered the place, all the assembled guests arose to greet him. But Daksha noticed that only his daughter and son-in-law remained seated. He was enraged at the sight and failed to realise that his son-in-law was the Supreme Lord, much above his stature. He decided to teach his son-in-law a lesson.

On returning to his palace after the completion of the yagna, Daksha decided he would host a grand yagna to which all the three worlds would be invited, except his ungrateful daughter and son-in-law. He made all suitable arrangements for the same, and the grand day arrived. Sati came to know that her father was hosting the yagna and decided to attend it. She wondered why she was not invited along with her husband, but her love for her father nudged her towards attending the yagna. She requested Lord Shiva to accompany her, but he refused. He said Daksha was doing this on purpose and it would not hold him in dignity if he visited the place without being invited. Since Sati kept insisting, he allowed her to go to the yagna protected with his attendants.

On reaching the venue, Sati found that there was no one to welcome her. Her father, Daksha, welcomed all the other guests but was oblivious to the fact that his daughter had also come. Sati felt humiliated that no one was taking notice of her. She argued with her father about the humiliation he was meting out to her and her husband, but in vain. She felt ashamed that she was born as a daughter to such a conceited king. She announced that she would cast off this body of hers that was given to her by Daksha and shall unite with her Lord in her rebirth. She immolated herself immediately.

Rebirth as Parvathi

Himavat, the king of the Himalayas, and his wife, Menadevi, were ardent devotees of Lord Shiva. Menadevi and Himavat underwent several years of penance invoking Shakthi. Shakthi, pleased with Menadevi and Himavat, blessed them with their desired boon of having 100 sons and a daughter (who would be an incarnation of Shakthi herself). They named the girl child Parvathi.

Parvathi, again, was a strong devotee of Lord Shiva and was always seen worshipping Lord Shiva. Parvathi resolved that she would win Lord Shiva and would marry none other.

Once, when Lord Shiva was meditating in the Himalayas, Parvathi served him with utmost devotion. Lord Kama, the God of Love, thought he should try to help her. He shot arrows of love at the meditating Shiva so that he would fall for Parvathi. Disturbed by Kama's arrows, the furious

Lord Shiva opened his 'third eye' and burnt him to ashes. He continued with his meditation. Parvathi undertook a severe penance to win over Lord Shiva. Parvathi's penance was so powerful that the Gods of all the three worlds were dumbstruck at the severity of her penance.

To test Parvathi's love for him, Lord Shiva disguised himself as an old man, rugged and fearsome in appearance, and appeared before her. Just as she was about to start her penance for the day, he came up to her and asked her the reason behind her prayers. She replied that she was doing it to win her Master - Lord Shiva. The 'old man' laughed aloud and commented that she was wasting her life for a mere ascetic who did not equal her in charm and beauty. Parvathi grew enraged at this comment and asked him to leave her sight immediately. She warned him of bad consequences if he spoke another disparaging word against her Lord.

Lord Shiva was pleased with her devotion and love towards him and appeared before her in his true form, agreeing to marry her. This was his Sati indeed, who had, true to her word, taken rebirth as Parvathi and come back to him.

Himavat was only too pleased to give his daughter's hand to one of the Supreme Lords and arranged for their marriage. After the marriage, Lord Shiva escorted his wife, Goddess Parvathi, to Kailasa. After a few years, the two became four, with Lord Ganesha and Lord Karthikeya forming part of the four-member family!

Shiva Parvathi Sloka:

Maata Cha Parvathi Devi, Pitaa Devo Maheshvara
Baandhavah Shiva Bhaktaacha, Svadesho Bhuvanatrayam.

Meaning:

Goddess Parvathi is the mother of all, and Lord Shiva is our Divine Father. Their devotees are all relatives. The world we live in is the creation of such divine beings.

Shiva and Shakthi – the names become one – in the form of 'Ardhanareeswara'. This form has two halves – one half of Shiva & the other half of Shakthi; indicative of the fact that men & women are equal.

Second in Line – The Koorma Avatar

It all began when the Devas and Asuras engaged in battles, and the Devas were being killed in large numbers. Lord Indra and his kingdom were also bereft of any wealth and auspiciousness, due to a curse by Sage Durvasa. The Devas ran to Lord Vishnu and asked him for protection. The Lord advised them to churn the 'Ocean of Milk' and drink the 'Amrit/Amritham' – Nectar of Immortality – that would arise from the churning. Since the ocean was huge, He asked the Devas to take the help of the Asuras (demons) also. He instructed them to use Mount Mandara as the churning stick and Vasuki, the King of Serpents, as the rope for churning.

The Asuras also agreed to help the Devas with the task on the condition that they would also partake of the Nectar of Immortality. But even as they started churning the ocean, the Devas and Asuras found that the mountain was too heavy and was sinking in the ocean. Noticing this, Lord Vishnu took the form of a huge tortoise ('Koorma') and bore the weight of Mount Mandara on His back. They were now successfully able to churn the Ocean of Milk, out of which Kamadhenu (the holy cow), Airavat (white elephant), Sri

Lakshmi, Varuni, Paarijatha Tree (the tree which fulfilled any wish), and a few more appeared. Finally, 'Dhanvanthri', the Physician God, appeared with the much-awaited 'Amrit/Amritham – Nectar of Immortality'.

The Asuras snatched the nectar and ran away to share it among themselves. Petrified, the Devas again turned to Lord Vishnu for help. The Lord was annoyed at the Asuras' betrayal and said he would help the Devas.

Lord Vishnu took the form of a beautiful damsel called 'Mohini' and appeared in front of the Asuras. The Asuras, who were fighting among themselves for the nectar, stopped at once at the sight of Mohini. Mesmerised by her beauty, they requested her to distribute the nectar to them. She said she would do so on one condition - they should accept her distribution unquestioningly. Sunk in her beauty, the Asuras accepted any condition she put forward.

Mohini requested the Devas and Asuras to sit in separate lines, and even as the Asuras sat in awe of her, she started distributing the nectar to the Devas. In their attempt to please Mohini, the Asuras did not bother to stop her from doing so. Only after the nectar was over did they realise that they had been tricked and waged a war against the Devas. Fresh from consuming the 'Nectar of Immortality', the Devas could not be defeated, and the Asuras had to retreat to the underworld!

Story of Raaghu

During the distribution of nectar to the Devas, an Asura called Raaghu transformed himself to look like a Deva and sat among the Devas. Unaware of this, Mohini had given him a part of the nectar. The Sun and Moon Gods figured this out and informed Mohini regarding the same. Lord Vishnu became furious and catapulted His 'Sudharshan Chakra' at the Asura, which split him into head and body. But since the Asura had already consumed the nectar, his head attained immortality. His trunk, to which the nectar did not reach, fell down dead. Lord Vishnu gave Raaghu the position of a planet since he had become immortal.

Legend has it that Raaghu shows his vengeance on the Sun and the Moon Gods by causing solar and lunar eclipses on the new moon day and the full moon day, respectively, whenever he gets an opportunity.

Story of the Neelkanth

During the churning, the ocean brought forth a deadly poison called Halahala. The effect of the poison spread in all directions, causing fear among all the creatures. They all prayed to Lord Shiva to help them. Lord Shiva appeared and swallowed the poison to protect the other mortals. The poison turned Lord Shiva's throat blue, which is why He came to be known as Neelkanth (the One with Blue Throat).

Koorma Sloka:

Sura-Asuraannaam-Udadhim Mathnataam Mandaraacalam
Dadhre Kamattha-Ruupenna Prssttha Ekaadashe Vibhuh

Meaning:

When the Suras (Devas) and the Asuras (Demons) were churning the Ocean with the Mandarachala mountain, the All-Pervading Lord supported that mountain on his back in the form of a Kamattha (Tortoise) during his eleventh incarnation.

BHISHMA – THE GRAND OLD MAN

Bhishma (Birth name - Devavrata) was the son of Shantanu, the King of Hastinapura, and Mother Ganga.

Birth of Devavrata

One day, King Shantanu - a descendant of the Lunar Dynasty, was taking a walk on the banks of the River Ganga when his eyes fell upon a beautiful damsel. He immediately fell in love with the beautiful woman and proposed that she marry him. The woman was none other than Ganga, and she agreed to marry him on one condition - that the king should never question any of her actions, or she would disappear. The King readily gave her his word that he would never interfere in her actions, and they soon got married.

Soon after their wedding, Ganga gave birth to a baby. The King's joy knew no bounds, but the joy was short-lived. Ganga took her baby, walked to the river, and drowned her baby there. The King was aghast at this behaviour of Ganga but could not question her since he had given her his word of non-interference. A few months later, Ganga gave birth to the second child, but repeated her action.

The King was again shocked by these happenings but could not bring himself to ask her. Ganga repeated this to seven of their children. The King was deeply anguished at the loss of the seven children and could not stop himself anymore. As she was about to drown their eighth child, the King stopped her and asked why she was behaving this way with their beloved children. To this, Ganga replied that she would tell him the reason but would depart from his place to her own abode.

The eight children of Shantanu and Ganga were the eight Vasus who had been cursed by Sage Vasishta because they stole his cow. He had cursed them that they would be born as mortals on earth, but after hearing their pleas, he relented and assured them that they would be freed from his curse within a year of their birth. He did not relax his curse on the 8th Vasu who stole the cow with the help of other Vasus, and this 8th Vasu had to live for a long time on earth - as Bhishma.

Ganga took with her their son, Devavrata, and made him an accomplished prince, tutoring him under the likes of Sage Vasishta and Sage Parashurama. She led the prince back to his father, Shantanu, to be crowned the Prince of Hastinapura. Shantanu was only too overjoyed to receive his son back and immediately crowned him prince.

Satyavati

King Shantanu, one day, noticed a woman on the banks of the River Yamuna and fell in love with her. He wanted to marry her and expressed this desire to her father - the Chief of Fisherfolk in their kingdom. Her father agreed on one condition - that Satyavati's son be declared as the heir to Hastinapura's throne. Taken aback by such a demand, Shantanu returned to his kingdom, unable to deprive Devavrata of his right.

Days passed, and Shantanu could not shake off his thoughts of Satyavati. He lost interest in his daily life and seemed to be drowned in despair. Devavrata noticed this and, from various sources, understood the reason behind his father's sadness. He made his way to Satyavati's house and spoke to her father, only to be faced with the same condition.

The Big Vow!

For the sake of his father, Devavrata immediately renounced his title as the Prince of Hastinapura and promised that Satyavati's son would ascend the throne. To this, Satyavati's father claimed that though he had given his word, Devavrata's children in the future may claim the right to the throne and thereby become a hindrance to Satyavati's children.

Without much ado, Devavrata immediately vowed that he would not marry and therefore there would be no children who could claim any rights to the throne. This vow of celibacy earned him the name 'Bhishma' - one who could fulfil a fierce oath.

As per the oath he gave to Satyavati's father, Bhishma led the life of a 'Brahmacharya' – a man who does not marry. He dedicated his life to serving the throne of Hastinapura, but for long the throne remained vacant. The mighty warrior that he was, no king was able to attack Hastinapura when the kingdom was under the care of the able Bhishma.

Bhishma's Brothers

Satyavati gave birth to two sons - Chitrangada and Vichitraveerya, and they grew up under the care and tutelage of their half-brother, Bhishma, since their father, King Shantanu, passed away. Soon after Chitrangada was crowned the King of Hastinapura, he died fighting against a Gandharva, and hence Bhishma consecrated Vichitraveerya to be the next king.

Bhishma decided to get Vichitraveerya married to a princess to beget children so that the throne of Hastinapura was guarded even after Vichitraveerya. He came to know about the Swayamvara of the three princesses of the King of Kasi - Amba, Ambika, and Ambalika and made his way to attend the same. He forcefully brought the three princesses, fighting against all the other kings who had assembled for the Swayamvara, to marry them off to Vichitraveerya. Bhishma was virtuous enough not to do this act for himself, but his devotion to the throne of Hastinapura and his intention to somehow create an heir to the throne made him take some hard decisions in his life, which he would have never made otherwise. However, upon reaching Hastinapura, Princess Amba declared that she was already in love with King Salva and had decided to marry only him. Bhishma immediately let Amba go free so that she could marry the person she liked and decided to get Ambika and Ambalika married to his brother.

This episode & Princess Amba's story is one of great importance in the life of Bhishma since she became the reason for Bhishma's death in her next birth.

A few years after the marriage took place, Vichitraveerya also died, leaving Hastinapura without an heir.

Satyavati, with the help of Sage Vyasa, invoked the practice of Niyoga, and thus three princes were born - Dhritarashtra, Pandu, and Vidura.

Bhishma's life spanned three generations, including himself & his nephews, Dhritarashtra, Pandu & Vidura, and the Pandavas and Kauravas. Throughout his life, his actions focused on protecting the throne in the absence of a king, on creating progeny so that the future of Hastinapura would be in safe hands, and on trying to reconcile between the two sets of cousins. He stood by his word and by the throne of Hastinapura - and did what it took to remain loyal to the throne. He protected his Dharma of keeping his word, but there were times he had to lean towards adharma to keep his word.

Upon learning the sacrifice his son had made for him, King Shantanu had granted him a boon - that he would live long and death could never near him unless he wished for it himself. True to this boon, Bhishma lived a long life, and though he did not ascend the throne of Hastinapura, he was always there for the throne to lean upon him!

PANCHAMUKHA – THE VAYUPUTRA

Lord Hanuman – The Son of Anjana and Kesari, is one of the most important Gods of the Hindu religion. He is known by other names such as Vayuputra (The Son of Vayu, the God of Air), Anjaneya (Son of Anjana), Maruthi (Son of Marut), and Pavanputra (Son of Pavan). Marut and Pavan are the other names of Vayu.

Lord Hanuman played an important role in the epic Ramayana as one of the ardent devotees of Lord Rama. His role in locating Sita, abducted by Ravana, the King of Lanka, and fighting the war against the demon king is of indisputable importance.

From the Ramayana

At a point in the Ramayana, Ravana ordered his brothers, Ahiravana and Mahiravana, to kill Lord Rama and his brother, Lakshmana. The demon brothers – Ahiravana and Mahiravana – attempted to kidnap Lord Rama & Lakshmana, but all their efforts were thwarted by Hanuman.

The demon brothers eventually resorted to disguising themselves as Vibhishana – the brother of Ravana who became a supporter of Lord Rama, so that they could get through Hanuman. They kidnapped Lord Rama & Lakshmana and hid them in their kingdom, Patala Loka (the underground world), which is inhabited only by demons. The demon brothers planned to use the unconscious Lord Rama & Lakshmana as a sacrificial offering to their Goddess.

In Search of the Lord

Aghast at the thought that he had allowed the kidnapping of his Lord, Hanuman immediately sought the help of Vibhishana, who guided him to Patala Loka.

At the gates of Patala Loka stood Makardhwaja, the gatekeeper. He appeared to be partly a Vanara (monkey) and partly a reptile. Makardhwaja conveyed that he was Hanuman's son, born out of the sweat dropped by Hanuman in the Lankan Ocean, which had entered a Makar (reptile). Hanuman blessed him and continued his journey towards finding his Lord.

After long searches, he finally located the unconscious brothers, Rama & Lakshmana. But Hanuman was in a fix; he could not rescue his Lord and Lakshmana unless Ahiravana and Mahiravana were killed. And to kill the demon brothers, he had to extinguish five lamps lit in different directions; the catch here was that he had to complete this at the same instant.

Panchamukha Anjaneya

Hanuman immediately assumed a form where he had five faces, each facing a different direction, so that he could blow the lamps simultaneously. The five faces were:

1. Hanuman – facing east
2. Narasimha – facing south

3.   Garuda – facing west
4.   Varaha – facing north
5.   Hayagriva – facing the sky

Hanuman, facing east, grants purity of mind and success. Narasimha, facing south, grants fearlessness. The west-facing Garuda removes black magic and poisons. The north-facing Varaha showers prosperity and wealth. Hayagriva, facing the sky, gives knowledge and good children.

Making use of the Panchamukha form (five faces), Hanuman was able to extinguish all the five flames at the same instant. This form is commonly known as Panchamukha Anjaneya or Panchamukhi Anjaneya. After defeating the demon brothers, Hanuman crowns Makardhwaja, the King of Patala Loka.

He revives Lord Rama and Lakshmana and flies them back to the battleground, where a fierce war ensues between Lord Rama's army and Ravana's army.

Anjaneya Sloka:

Budhdirbalam, yaso' dhairyam, Nirbhayatva-maro'gata |
Ajadatyam, Vakpatutvam ca, Hanumatsmaranadbhavet ||

Meaning:

Wisdom (budhi), physical strength (balam), fame (yashas), courage (dhairyam), fearlessness (nirbhayam), good health (arogata), vigilance (ajadatyam), eloquence in speech (vakpatutvam) are bestowed upon us on bowing to Lord Hanuman.

Varaha Avatar – The Third Avatar

Lord Brahma's four sons once decided to visit Lord Vishnu at Vaikund to seek his blessings. Sanaka, Sanatana, Sanandana and Sanatkumara (together known as ChathurSana - the four Sanas) were stopped by the guards at Vaikund - Jay and Vijay. Furious at being denied entry to see the Lord, the four sons cursed the Dwara Balakas (guards at the entrance) to be born as demons on earth.

Knowing what had happened, Lord Vishnu himself stepped out and apologised to the ChathurSana. They said they would not repeal the curse but mentioned that the two demons would undergo the curse and then return to Lord Vishnu himself. The two guards were thus born on earth as Hiranyaksha and Hiranyakashipu.

In the meanwhile, while Lord Brahma was busy in the work of creation, Bhooma Devi (Mother Earth) had submerged in the ocean. Lord Brahma meditated on Lord Vishnu to protect the world and its beings. It was probably time for the Lord to manifest Himself on earth. As Lord Brahma meditated, a tiny boar flew out of his nostrils and grew to the size of a mountain. The boar was none other than Lord Vishnu.

The boar (Varaha in Sanskrit) dived deep into the ocean, lifted Bhoomadevi, and placed her on the waters.

Around the same time, Hiranyaksha, the mighty and arrogant Asura, went to heaven seeking war. However, Lord Indra and his Gods hid themselves, scared to face Hiranyaksha. Hiranyaksha then went up to the Lord of Waters, Varuna, seeking to fight with him. Varuna did not want to engage in a fight with Hiranyaksha, so he sent Hiranyaksha to Lord Vishnu. Hiranyaksha went looking for Lord Vishnu and found Him in the form of a boar (Varaha) holding up Bhoomadevi with the tip of His tusks. When challenged to a fight by the Asura, Varaha placed Bhoomadevi on the water and indulged in a severe battle against the demon Hiranyaksha. The battle is said to have lasted for a long while. Finally, Lord Vishnu as Varaha Avatar killed the demon.

The demon Hiranyakashipu was later killed by Lord Vishnu in the form of Narasimha.

Varaha Sloka:

Sthite manasi suswasthe sareere sati yo narah.
Dhaatu saamye sthite smartaa viswaroopam cha maam ahjam.
Tatas thum mriyamaanam, tu kaashta-paashaana sannibham
Aham smaraami mad bhaktam, nayaami paramaam gatim.

Meaning:

A person who has a healthy mind and body, when he realises Me - as the one without birth or death, I remember to liberate him as he reaches his last moments.

Vidura – An Incarnation of Lord Dharma

Vidura – the third grandson of Shantanu & Satyavati (his elder brothers were Dhritarashtra & Pandu), was a wise man renowned for his knowledge, intelligence and virtues all over the world.

Sage Mandavya

Sage Mandavya was a hermit who practiced meditation for a good number of years and possessed strong yogic powers. One day, when he was immersed in his daily prayers, a band of robbers was being chased by the king's soldiers. The robbers found the hermit's cottage nearby and thought it would be an ideal place to hide their booty. They went in and hid their booty in a corner and hid themselves elsewhere.

The soldiers, tracking the robbers by their footprints, came upon Sage Mandavya's Ashram. They enquired about the robbers, but he did not respond as he was observing the vow of silence. The soldiers barged into the cottage and found the booty. Assuming that the sage was part of the robbery (since he kept silent for every question, and they found the booty in his place), the soldiers promptly brought the robbers and the sage to the king. The king ordered his soldiers to execute the robbers and the sage at once. The soldiers promptly carried out the king's orders and executed the hermit.

But Sage Mandavya, all-powerful through his years of asceticism, did not lose his life. Instead, he called upon Dharma, the Lord of Justice, and put forth his query to him. He questioned Lord Dharma as to why this kind of tragedy had befallen him. To this, Lord Dharma quietly replied that it was a result of one of his past actions. He explained that Sage Mandavya had pierced an insect when he was a child and had to bear the consequence now.

The Curse

On hearing this, Sage Mandavya grew furious. He was being punished for a crime that was committed out of ignorance at a very early age. He cursed Lord Dharma that he would be born as a human being on earth for inflicting such an undeserving punishment.

Birth as Vidura

Thus, Lord Dharma came to earth as a mortal and was born as Vidura. His birth was conceived under unusual circumstances - born into a royal family but not of royal blood. Neither of his parents (Sage Vyasa and the maid of Ambalika) were of royal blood, and hence he was not considered to ascend the throne of Hastinapura despite his wisdom and other virtues.

An interesting fact to note is that, while Vidura was an incarnation of Lord Dharma, Yudhishthira – the eldest of the Pandavas and the son of Pandu & Kunti, was the son of Lord Dharma (as Yudhishthira was born by Kunti invoking Lord Dharma using her Mantra).

KARTHIKEYA – THE SON OF THE NEELKANTH

L ord Karthikeya, the second son of Lord Shiva and Goddess Parvathi, is known as the God of War and Victory.

The Wait for a Saviour

Maya, a demoness, transformed herself into a beautiful woman and married Sage Kashyapa, not revealing her identity to him. Her intent was to give birth to children who would rule over the three worlds, since they would be born with yogic powers from the sage. Maya and Sage Kashyapa gave birth to three sons – Surapadma, Simhamukha, and Taraka.

The Asuras (demons) – Surapadma, Simhamukha and Taraka – were ambitious to take over the throne of Indra and rule the three worlds. Having understood the power of the Devas, they devised plans to obtain boons first before they attacked the Devas. The brothers performed severe penance and won boons from Lord Shiva that they cannot be defeated by any power other than Lord Shiva's.

With growing arrogance, the Asuras started terrorising the Devas and Rishis (godly men). They aimed at conquering the Devas and ruling over them by seizing the throne from Indra

(King of the Devas). With their immense power, the Asuras captured and imprisoned many of the Devas. The Devas ran to Lord Shiva for help, having realised that He was the only person who could save them from Surapadma, Simhamukha and Taraka. This was exactly the time when Shiva had remarried Shakthi, in the form of Goddess Parvathi.

The Birth of Karthikeya

Realising that he had to do something about the Asuras, Lord Shiva opened his Third Eye, out of which six divine sparks arose and handed them over to Agni, the God of Fire. Agni took the sparks with him and left them in River Ganga. The flowing river carried the sparks up to the Shravan, forest of reeds (Shara – Reeds; Van – Forest). It was here that the six sparks turned into six beautiful babies in lotuses. The Kritika women, again six in number, found these babies and each of these women took care of one child.

The babies merged to form one boy with six heads – Lord Karthikeya.

The boy came to be known as Shravan, since he was born in Shravan; as Karthikeya, as he was brought up by the Kritika women; as Shanmuga & Aarumuga, as he had six faces.

The End of the Asura Trio

At the appropriate time, Lord Shiva called upon Karthikeya and asked him to vanquish the Asura brothers, Surapadma, Simhamukha & Taraka. Lord Shiva appointed Veerabahu as the chief of Karthikeya's army and Goddess Parvathi gifted him with the divine spear (Vel). With his parents' blessings, Karthikeya left the abode with the motive of liberating the Devas. After fierce battles with the Asura brothers & their army, Karthikeya emerged victorious after defeating the three Asura brothers, with the help of his chief & loyalist, Veerabahu. The story, which says that Lord Shiva granted them boons of immortality, believes that Surapadma took two forms, one as a Peacock (Karthikeya's Vaahan/Vehicle) and the other as a Cock (the emblem in Karthikeya's flag), thereby ensuring he did not die.

Marriage with Devasena

Indra was pleased with Lord Karthikeya on his victory over the Asuras. As a token of gratitude for having restored the dignity of the Devas, Indra offered his daughter, Devasena's (Deivayanai) hand to Lord Karthikeya and requested him to accept her as his wife. Lord Karthikeya willingly accepted, and the marriage took place in Thiruparankundram amidst much splendour.

Marriage with Valli

Lord Vishnu was once born as a hermit, and Goddess Lakshmi was born as a beautiful deer, which attracted the attention of the hermit. At the same time, a pious girl by the name of Sundaravalli performed penance to marry Lord Karthikeya. Pleased by her penance, Lord Karthikeya asked her to enter the womb of the deer, which she did. The deer gave birth to the child in a deep pit dug on the ground. The chief of the tribe, Nambi, and his wife found the baby and decided to raise the baby as their daughter. They named their daughter Valli ('Vallikizhangu' is a type of vegetable that is grown underground; since Valli was found in a pit dug up, she was named so) and brought her up with love and affection.

Years passed by, and Valli grew up to be a beautiful woman. Once, when Valli was out watching over the fields, an old man approached her for food. As kind as she was, Valli offered him some fruits and water. The old man thanked her and told her that he was in love with her. Valli refused his proposal. The old man was actually Lord Karthikeya, who had come in disguise to tease Valli. He immediately invoked his elder brother, Lord Ganesha, to help him out, and Lord Ganesha appeared in the form of an elephant. The sight of the elephant terrified Valli, and she ran to the old man, requesting him to save her. At that time, the Lord regained his true form and revealed his identity to her. Valli was only too pleased to behold Lord Karthikeya in his true form and fell in love with Him.

Nambi also agreed to give his daughter's hand to the Lord, and the marriage was held in pomp and show, with the Gods showering their blessings on the young couple.

Devasena and Valli were the daughters of Lord Vishnu in their previous births, named Amritavalli & Sundaravalli. They were eager to wed Lord Karthikeya and thus performed severe penance to win him over. He granted them the boon of marriage in their next births, which is why the Lord had two wives.

Kartikeya Sloka:

Om Thatpurushaya Vidhmahe, Maha Senaya Dhimahi
Thannah Shanmukha Prachodhayath

Meaning:

Let us know the Supreme Being and meditate upon Him, the Supreme General of the great Deva Army- Lord Shanmuga (Skanda). May He enlighten us and lead us to be one with Him.

Six hills in the state of Tamil Nadu, India, have been fortunate to be the chosen abode for Lord Karthikeya. The places are listed below in the order of his life's events:

1. Pazhani – the hill where Lord Karthikeya resigned himself to, as a child, over a fight with his elder brother, Lord Ganesha, for a mango
2. Swamimalai – where Lord Karthikeya, as a young learned boy, preached the meaning of the divine word 'Om' to his father, Lord Shiva
3. Thiruchendur – where he won the battle against the Asura brothers (Surapadma, Simhamukha and Taraka)
4. Thiruparangundram – the hill where he married Goddess Devasena, the daughter of Indra
5. Thirutthani – the hill where he married Goddess Valli, the daughter of Nambi
6. Pazhamudhircholai – where he gives his darshan to devotees with Devasena and Valli

NARASIMHA AVATAR – THE FOURTH AVATAR

When the news of Lord Varaha annihilating the demon Hiranyaksha fell on his brother Hiranyakashipu's ears, the latter grew furious. He vowed revenge against Lord Vishnu for killing his brother.

He went into deep penance in the valley of Mount Mandara to obtain the boon of invincibility from Lord Brahma. The Lord was pleased with his years of penance and granted him a boon. Hiranyakashipu requested the Lord that he should not meet death indoors or outdoors, on the earth or in the sky, in the morning or at night, by a man or by an animal, by hand or by any weapon - thus ensuring he could not die at all. The Lord, however, granted him this boon.

Soon after obtaining this boon, Hiranyakashipu began his tyranny and oppressed all three worlds. His torments were becoming difficult for the Devas, and they pleaded with Lord Vishnu to help them out.

Bhaktha Prahlad

On the other hand, Hiranyakashipu's wife, Kayadhu, had given birth to a son - whom they named Prahlad. He grew up to be an ardent devotee of Lord Vishnu, against his father's wishes.

The story goes that when Hiranyakashipu was performing his penance for many years, the Devas took the opportunity to attack the demon world. However, Sage Narada intervened and saved Hiranyakashipu's wife, who was then carrying the little one. Sage Narada then took her to his hermitage. When she was under his care, Sage Narada used to sing in praise of Lord Vishnu and tell her stories of the great Lord. The unborn baby also listened to these praises of the Lord, and that was the reason Prahlad grew up to be an ardent devotee even though his father was against the Lord.

Hiranyakashipu tried to dissuade Prahlad from worshipping Lord Vishnu; however, he remained as staunch as anyone could be. Hiranyakashipu's vanity took over his fatherly love, and he went to great lengths to stop his son from continuing to worship the Lord. He asked his guards to set elephants on his son, but it was the elephants that got injured. Prahlad was also thrown into a blazing fire, but the fire couldn't harm Prahlad.

Rise of the Lion God

One day, Hiranyakashipu confronted his son. He mockingly asked where his God was. Prahlad replied, "The Lord is Omnipresent. He is present in this pillar as well." Hiranyakashipu went and thrashed the pillar nearby to prove that there was no Lord in the pillar.

However, as the pillar cracked into two - Lord Narasimha, the fourth Avatar of Lord Vishnu, arose from the pillar.

The upper half of his body was that of a lion, and his lower half was that of a man (He was neither an animal nor a man). He charged at the demon and carried him to the door of the assembly hall (neither indoors nor outdoors), placed him on his lap (neither on earth nor in the sky), and dug his nails (neither by hand nor with any weapon) into Hiranyakashipu's body and killed him that evening (neither morning nor night).

It took a long time before Narasimha could return to a calm state - he stayed in a state of wrath even after the Devas bowed and prayed to him. However, when his devotee Prahlad prayed with love and devotion, Narasimha softened and blessed him. Prahlad was made the next king after his father, and he ruled his kingdom virtuously for many years.

Narasimha Sloka:

Ugram viram maha-vishnum
Jvalantam sarvato mukham
Narasimham bhishanam bhadram.
Mrityur mrityum namamy aham!!

Meaning:

"I bow down to Lord Narasimha, who is ferocious and heroic like Lord Vishnu.

He is burning from every side. He is terrific, auspicious and. the death of death personified."

KUNTI – THE MOTHER OF SIX

Kunti, one of the prominent queens in the Mahabharata, was the daughter of King Kuntibhoja, the wife of King Pandu, and the mother of six - Karna and the five brothers, the Pandavas.

Birth of Kunti

Kunti was born to Shurasena, a Yadava king, and was named Pritha. She was given in adoption to King Kuntibhoja, who renamed her Kunti, the name by which she came to be known thereafter.

Kunti was the sister of Vasudeva (the father of Lord Krishna), which is why the Pandavas were known to be cousins of Krishna.

The Rarest of Rare Mantras

Kunti was brought up with a lot of love and affection by Kuntibhoja, and she grew up into a beautiful girl. When she was young, Sage Durvasa visited their kingdom. Because the sage was known for his wrath and powerful curses, King Kuntibhoja made sure all arrangements were in place to make the Sage feel comfortable during his stay in the kingdom. Kunti spent all her time with Sage Durvasa and helped him complete his rituals with complete devotion and spirit. Sage Durvasa was extremely pleased and satisfied with her commitment and blessed her by teaching her a rare 'Mantra'. The recital of the Mantra would allow Kunti to invoke any God of her choice and beget children with his blessings.

Birth of Karna

Having been taught a very powerful mantra, something which was almost unbelievable, the young Kunti was intrigued as to whether it would really work. Not out of her childlike behaviour yet, the young princess chanted the mantra invoking Lord Surya (the Sun God). Immediately, the God appeared before her and blessed her with a baby boy, Karna. The baby boy was born with a Kavasa (armour) and a pair of Kundalas (earrings), which had great powers associated with them. Kunti was totally taken aback as she did not expect this to happen. The problem being, she was still unmarried, and she could not bring disgrace to her family. With a heavy heart, she decided to abandon the baby by placing him in a casket and letting him float in a river.

Marriage with Pandu

As years passed, Kunti came to be known as one of the most eligible women in the country, far surpassing others in beauty and wisdom. Her father arranged a Swayamvara (an ancient practice in India, where all eligible bridegrooms are invited and the bride gets to choose her husband, according to her preferences), where almost all the princes had assembled, eager to win the heart of the beautiful princess.

Of the many princes, Kunti chose the Prince of Hastinapura, Pandu and married him. Pandu later married Madri, the princess of Madra.

After a few years of palace life, King Pandu retired to the forests with his two queens.

One day, Pandu went for a hunting expedition deep into the forests. He spotted a deer and shot his arrow at it. The arrow found its mark, and the deer fell to the ground. A few minutes later, Pandu realised that he had killed Sage Chintamani, who had taken the form of a deer while he was enjoying his time with his mate.

Pandu ran towards the dying Sage, fell at his feet and begged his pardon. The sage, in his last moments of life, was enraged at the sight of Pandu. He cursed Pandu that he would also die in a similar situation. Pandu was crestfallen at this curse and prayed to the sage to forgive him but in vain. Pandu returned to his queens and narrated the happenings to them. All three of them were broken since they did not have even one child until then.

The Birth of the Pandavas

It was during this time that Kunti confided in Pandu about the mantra Sage Durvasa had taught her and the power of the mantra. Pandu was only too overjoyed on hearing this and said they should beget children with the help of the mantra. First, they called upon Lord Dharma (God of Justice) using the mantra and were blessed with Yudhishthira, as righteous as the God himself. Next, they called upon Lord Vayu (God of Air) to bless them with a child as strong as Vayu. Thus, Bhima, the strongest of all the princes, was born. For their third son, the couple invoked Lord Indra (King of Devas), who blessed them with Arjuna, second to none other than Indra himself in fame & valour.

Pandu requested Kunti to share the mantra with Madri too. Kunti obliged his request and taught Madri the mantra. Pandu & Madri invoked the Ashwini Brothers to bless them with children, because of which Nakula & Sahadeva, the twin brothers, were born.

Death of Pandu

Years passed, and the Pandava princes grew up to be handsome young boys. They stuck to their virtues of justice, strength and valour. One day, when Pandu neared Madri, she warned him about the curse from the Sage Kindamamuni a few years back. But Pandu paid no heed to her words. The effect of the curse was still alive, and Pandu died instantaneously. Madri, who was taken over by guilt that her husband died because of her, did not want to live anymore and joined her husband on his journey to heaven. Kunti, on the other hand, was left to take care of their five sons.

She returned to Hastinapura with her five sons so that they could be taken care of appropriately with the help of Bhishma,

Vidura and their kith & kin. The Pandava princes did not find favour with their cousins, the Kaurava princes (sons of Dhritarashtra, the elder brother of Pandu). They were constantly harassed by the 100 Kaurava princes, primarily Duryodhana, the eldest among them. Even from early childhood, the minds of the Kaurava princes were poisoned by Shakuni, the brother-in-law of Dhritarashtra, who instilled in them the belief that they should be the successors to the throne of Hastinapura. As they grew into young men, the hatred between the two sides continued to escalate. This ultimately led to the terrible Battle of Kurukshetra, the war between Dharma & Adharma. In the war, her first son, Karna - born of the Sun God, took the side of Duryodhana and was killed by the Pandavas, leaving Kunti with feelings of guilt and sadness.

Death of Kunti

The Pandavas, who followed the path of Dharma, won the battle, and Yudhishthira ascended the throne. Dhritarashtra & Gandhari, the parents of the Kaurava princes, retired to the forests, renouncing worldly pleasures. Kunti, also weary of her difficult life, accompanied them to the forests. During their ascetic life, all three of them died due to a forest fire.

The life of a queen, who fought with difficult situations throughout her life, right from Karna's birth and his abandonment, dealing with her husband's curse, his death, parenting five children single-handedly, and protecting them from their villainous cousins, to facing Karna's death at the hands of her own children, thus ended.

VAMANA AVATAR – THE FIFTH ONE

King Mahabali was the son of King Virochana and the grandson of King Prahlad (the devotee whom Lord Vishnu saved from Hiranyakashipu in his fourth Avatar).

Mahabali was a good king and a devotee of Lord Vishnu. As he was desirous of conquering the heavens, he performed the Viswajit sacrifice and received a golden chariot and celestial weapons from the sacrificial fire. Soon after, Mahabali proceeded to attack the Devas in the heavens. However, the Devas, realising that Mahabali was invincible at the moment, vacated the heavens. Thus, Mahabali began to rule the three worlds with the help of his Guru, Shukracharya.

Birth of Vamana Avatar

The Devas felt deprived, and Lord Indra was saddened at losing his kingdom. Aditi, the mother of the Devas, prayed to Lord Vishnu to restore the dignity of the Devas. Lord Vishnu said he would be born as her son to relieve the Devas of their pain. He was soon born to Aditi and Sage Kashyap as 'Vamana' – a dwarf-like boy.

As advised by Shukracharya, Mahabali was performing a series of Ashwamedha Yagnas. During one such Yagna, Vamana presented himself to Mahabali - who welcomed him and offered to give him anything that he asked for as alms, as that was the practice during Yagnas. Vamana requested three steps of land, which Mahabali readily agreed to give, much against the wishes of the suspicious Shukracharya, who understood the inner designs of Lord Vishnu.

As soon as he consented, Vamana grew in size, even bigger than the earth. He placed his first step on the earth to claim it for himself. He placed his second step in the heavens, thereby reclaiming Lord Indra's lost kingdom. He asked Mahabali where he could place his third step, to which Mahabali offered his head as he could not go back on his word of providing three steps to the dwarf-boy.

Lord Vishnu was impressed by how Mahabali did not swerve from the truth and kept his word, even when he was deprived of all his wealth. Lord Vishnu blessed Mahabali to rule as Indra in the Sutala region, a part of Patala Loka. This Avatar derives its uniqueness from the fact that it is the first Avatar that does not kill any wicked Asura, instead just banishes a king to restore the kingdom back to the Devas.

It is still believed that the King visits the earth once a year to check on his subjects - the day that is widely celebrated as Onam, where people welcome him with Pookolams and festive spreads.

Vamana Sloka:

Hemadri Shikarakaram,
Shudha Spatika Sannibham,

Poorna Chandra Nibhanam,
Devam Dwibujam, Vamanam Smareth ||

Meaning:

The one who has the form of a golden mountain,

The one who resembles pure crystal,

The one whose face looks like a full moon.

I bow down to you with both my hands!

SHANTHA – THE LONE PRINCESS

The epic, Ramayana, is primarily based on the Seventh Avatar of Lord Vishnu, Lord Rama, where the Lord assumes the life of a human and shows us the right path to be followed.

Lord Rama (son of Queen Kausalya) is known to have three younger brothers – Bharatha (son of Queen Kaikeyi) and Lakshmana & Shatrughana (sons of Queen Sumitra). Not known to many, Lord Rama also had a sister, by the name of Shantha – born to Dasharatha & Kausalya.

Early Life of Dasharatha

Dasharatha was born to King Aja of the Solar Dynasty, who ruled the Southern parts of the Kosala Kingdom. His mother was Indumathi, an Apsara (a celestial nymph) born on earth due to a curse. After her curse was lifted, Indumathi flew back to the heavens. Following this, King Aja also died, grief-stricken by her absence.

Dasharatha grew up under the care of the able minister, Sumanthra, and ascended the throne of Southern Kosala when it was the right time. He insisted on marrying Kausalya, the daughter of the King of Northern Kosala. The King of

Northern Kosala – Dakshina, agreed to give his daughter's hand to Dasharatha, and the wedding was solemnised to take place in a few days.

Abduction by Ravana

Ravana, the prince of Lanka, had called on Lord Brahma after severe penance to seek the boon of immortality. Lord Brahma, however, advised him to drop such thoughts as death was inevitable and his death would lie in the hands of the offspring of Dasharatha & Kausalya.

Fearing his death, Ravana wanted to kill Kausalya, but was stopped by his wife Mandodari, who advised him against committing the big sin of 'Stree Hati' (killing of a woman). This made him arrive at the conclusion that if Dasharatha & Kausalya were forbidden from marrying, they could have no children.

He then abducted Kausalya, put her in a box, and let the box float in a river, assuming that she would die. However, Dasharatha found the box at the right time and saved her life. Immediate arrangements were made for their marriage, and the wedding ceremony was conducted in great pomp.

Birth of Shantha

Soon after their marriage, Kausalya gave birth to a girl child – whom they named Shantha. However, to their horror, the child she had given birth to was handicapped.

It was advised that if Shantha was left in the custody of divine people, she would lose her handicap and regain normalcy. Thus, it was decided that Shantha would be adopted by Romapada, the King of Angadesa. The wife of Romapada, Varshini, was the sister of Kausalya. Hence, Shantha was actually given in adoption to her maternal aunt & uncle. Under the able care of the religious couple, Shantha was soon cured of her deformities and grew into a beautiful girl, well-versed in the Vedas & Arts.

Shantha's Marriage

Once, King Romapada incurred the wrath of Lord Indra, the King of the Devas, who cursed that his kingdom would not have any monsoon that season. Unable to see the plight of his citizen farmers, the king called upon Maharishi Rishyasringa to perform a Yagna that would bring rains to his kingdom.

After the successful completion of the Yagna, the kingdom received enough rainfall. The king could not thank the Maharishi enough and proposed the marriage of his daughter to him. Maharishi Rishyasringa agreed, and the marriage between him and Shantha was held amidst festivities.

Maharishi Rishyasringa was the Rishi who performed the Putrakameshti Yagna, held by Dasharatha, to beget sons as heirs to his kingdom. Lord Rama, Bharatha, Lakshmana, and Shatrughana were born after this Yagna.

THE BIRTH OF LORD RAMA

King Dasharatha ruled the kingdom of Ayodhya for many years with great name and fame. Assisted by an able set of ministers, his kingdom was a home for the happy and prosperous. He toiled for the well-being of his subjects and ruled with great ability.

His kingdom was a heaven for all but unhappy for one reason – they had no prince to succeed this great king. King Dasharatha had three queens – Kausalya, Kaikeyi, and Sumithra. He decided to conduct the Ashwamedh Yagna, which would please the Gods and may result in the birth of a prince to succeed him.

Putrakameshti Yagna

Preparations for the Ashwamedh Yagna were in full swing in the kingdom, and the King invited the great Sage Rishyashringa to perform this sacred Yagna. The Yagna was performed with all reverence, and towards the end of the successful completion of the Yagna, Sage Rishyashringa suggested performing the Putrakameshti Yagna, which would bless him with sons. The king readily agreed and performed this Yagna too with utmost devotion.

Upon completion of the Putrakameshti Yagna, a divine figure arose out of the sacrificial fire and handed over a golden vessel filled with Paayasam/Kheer (a sweet dish) to the King. He suggested that the King share the contents of this vessel among his three queens, and all three of them would give birth to sons.

The King was only too overjoyed to follow the instructions. He was eager to have a son who would be the future ruler of the kingdom and his subjects. He immediately shared the Paayasam with his queens.

Birth of the Divine

In due course, the three queens gave birth. Queen Kausalya gave birth to Rama, Queen Kaikeyi gave birth to Bharatha, and Queen Sumithra gave birth to twins - Lakshmana and Shatrughana (since she had two shares of the Paayasam).

The day Queen Kausalya gave birth to Lord Rama – the ninth day of Shukla Paksha in the month of Chaithra – is today celebrated as a festival, Rama Navami!

PARASURAMA AVATAR – THE ANGRY BIRD

Parasurama Avatar was the sixth Avatar of Lord Vishnu. The word 'Parasu' means 'Axe' - he was 'The Rama with an Axe'.

Lord Vishnu decided to appear in this Avatar to free the world from the Kshatriya kings who had started misusing their powers and abusing their subjects.

Birth of Parasurama

Lord Parasurama was born to Sage Jamadagni, a Brahmin, and Renuka, a Kshatriya woman. He imbibed many Kshatriya qualities and was therefore a fierce warrior.

Parasurama's father, Sage Jamadagni, owned a celestial cow named Kamadhenu, which could fulfil anyone's wishes. Kshatriya King Kartavirya Arjuna heard about this cow and wanted to own it. The king ordered his forces to take away the cow by force from Sage Jamadagni's house. On hearing this news, Parasurama grew furious and set out on a mission to rescue Kamadhenu. He challenged the evil King to fight with him and killed him in the ensuing battle. He returned home with the cow, but Sage Jamadagni was only too disappointed that his son had committed a crime which no Brahmin was supposed to do - killing someone. He asked his son to atone for his sin by going on a pilgrimage. Parashurama spent one year visiting holy places and returned to his hermitage.

The 21 Battles

Once, when Parasurama had left the hermitage for a while, Kartavirya's sons used the opportunity of Parasurama's absence to avenge their father's death. They killed the Sage. When Parasurama returned, he was shocked to learn about his father's death and the reason behind it. He vowed to take revenge for this unfair killing of his father. He decided to wipe out the entire Kshatriya race from the world to avenge his father's death. He fought 21 battles in succession to destroy the race and finally gave up after his ancestor, Sage Bhrigu, called upon him and requested him to give up his mission as the world was now free from the Kshatriyas who abused their power. Known for his obedience, Lord Parasurama obliged his ancestor's request and gave up his weapons.

Lord Parasurama is the only Avatar who lives through some of the next Avatars of Vishnu as well.

1. He makes an appearance in the Ramayana when he challenges Lord Rama (the Seventh Avatar) to a fight.
2. He also makes his presence felt in the Mahabharata - where Lord Krishna (Ninth Avatar) plays a pivotal role. He was the mentor to stalwarts like Bhishma, Drona and Karna.

Parasurama Sloka:

Kshatriya-rudhira-maye jagad-apagata-pâpam.
Snapayasi payasi s'amita-bhava-tâpam.
Kes'ava dhrita-bhrigupati-rûpa ||

Meaning:

The one who freed us from the tyrannous Kshatriya rulers and cleansed the world's sins,

The one who destroyed the world's anguish,

We hail you, Kesava, the Lord of the Bhrigus!

DRUPADA & DRONA – FRIENDSHIP TO ENMITY

'Drupada', the crown prince of Panchala, and 'Drona', the son of Sage Bharadwaj, were both students of Sage Bharadwaj. Drupada and Drona grew into thick friends during their time at the Gurukul where they underwent education. During a conversation, Drupada promised to Drona that once he returned to Panchala and was crowned the king, his palace would also be home to Drona.

Days passed, and the boys graduated from their Gurukul as young men, ready to face the world. Drupada returned to his kingdom and was crowned the King of Panchala, whereas Drona married and begot a son named Ashwatthama. Drona's family had to live in extreme poverty and Drona was determined to do something about it.

Recollecting the promise Drupada made to him, Drona embarked on a journey to Panchala to meet his friend. But lo! He failed to realise that Drupada was no longer just his friend but also the protector of his kingdom. Drupada declared that the promise was made at a very young age, when its consequences were not known and could not be honoured now, as the duty of a king forbade him to do so. Drona returned empty-handed but was determined to avenge the insult heaped on him and the dishonouring of the promise.

Guru for the Kurus

Drona was appointed by Bhishma to train the Kuru princes (the Pandavas and Kauravas). Drona went on to tutor all of them; however, Arjuna (the third of the Pandava princes) remained his favourite student because of his skills. Towards the end of the tutoring period, when the time for Guru Dakshina was near, Drona summoned all the princes and asked them to capture Drupada for his Guru Dakshina.

Drupada – Captured and Released!

Duryodhana, the eldest of the Kauravas, sprang to action and said he would accomplish the task for his Guru. However, the Kauravas were soon overpowered by Drupada. Next, Arjuna tried his hand at capturing Drupada and succeeded. He led Drupada to Drona and offered the Guru Dakshina that his Guru had asked for. Drona set Drupada free but retained one half of the kingdom. He gave the other half of the kingdom to Drupada as a mark of their friendship.

Revenge

Even as the defeated Drupada returned to his kingdom, he vowed to avenge the insults he had borne. He performed a grand Yagna and begot the twins – Dhrishtadyumna and Draupadi out of this fire, solely for the purpose of destroying Drona. During the Mahabharata war, Drupada & Dhrishtadyumna had teamed with the Pandavas (Draupadi married the Pandavas), the alliance which led to the defeat of the Kauravas. During the war, on the 14th day, Drona killed Drupada. Acting on his father's vow, Dhrishtadyumna killed Drona in the war. Drona's son, Ashwatthama, killed Dhrishtadyumna to avenge his father's death.

Drona was unconquerable by his opponents. But he had to be vanquished because he had taken the wrong path and the wrong side by supporting the Kauravas. He had to be killed by making him lay down his arms. Sri Krishna devised a plan and according to it, Bhima (the Second Pandava Prince) killed an elephant named Ashwatthama and proclaimed in the battlefield that he had killed Ashwatthama. Their plan was to make Drona believe that his son was dead and lay down his weapons. But Drona did not believe Bhima's words and questioned Yudhishthira (the eldest Pandava Prince) on whether his son was dead. He knew that Yudhishthira would never lie in his lifetime. The eldest prince replied that Ashwatthama was dead, but added indistinctly that it was Ashwatthama, the elephant. Hearing this, Drona laid down his weapons to meditate. This gave Dhrishtadyumna a chance to kill the great sage.

What began as a playful promise in childhood thus ended in multiple deaths in Drona's and Drupada's lineage due to the feeling of revenge. This friendship turned enmity between Drona and Drupada is a lesson for us from the Mahabharat that revenge and hatred would only result in self-destruction!

RAMA AVATAR

The chronology of the six Avatars of Lord Vishnu follows the pattern of the evolution of mankind. And the Seventh Avatar - Lord Rama – is where the evolution reaches the stage of a human being.

Lord Rama was born to the King of Ayodhya - Dasharatha and his Queen Kausalya. He was the first of the King's four sons - Rama (born to Queen Kausalya), Bharatha (born to Queen Kaikeyi), and Lakshmana & Shatrughana (the twins born to Queen Sumitra).

The four brothers grew up under the tutelage of the great Sage Vasishta.

Once, Sage Vishwamitra visited the King and requested him to send his son Rama with him to the forests to put an end to the demons who were a hindrance to his prayers and rituals. Though Dasharatha was not inclined to send his son and offered to go himself, the Sage declined the offer. Finally, the King gave in, and Rama and Lakshmana were instructed to accompany the Sage and serve him as needed. They set out on the mission to help the Sage complete his Yagna, and this was accomplished after the princes killed demons like Tataka, and also flung her son Maricha into the sea, 100 miles away.

The Four Weddings!

Once, Sage Vishwamitra led the princes to the kingdom of Mithila which was ruled by Janaka. The Sage described to Rama and Lakshmana about Lord Shiva's bow that was in the possession of King Janaka at Mithila, which the two brothers wished to see. At Mithila, the King mentioned that he had resolved to get his daughter, Princess Sita, married to the person who would be able to string Lord Shiva's bow. Many kings came to Mithila seeking Sita's hand, but none of them could string the bow. However, Prince Rama could easily pick the bow and as he tried to string it, the bow broke into two. King Janaka, witnessing Rama's feat, decided to get Sita married to him. The marriage of Rama and Sita was conducted in a grand manner. This was also followed by the marriage of Lakshmana with Urmila (Sita's sister), Bharatha with Mandvi (Sita's cousin), and Shatrughana with Shrutakirti (Sita's cousin).

The Crown Prince

The newly married couple lived happily in the city of Ayodhya until Dasharatha decided that he needed to choose the King-to-be. He announced that he would soon make his eldest son, Rama, the Crown Prince of Ayodhya. The city erupted in joy, and celebrations began. His three mothers were happy that their son was going to be the Crown Prince. But there was one person, Manthara, Queen Kaikeyi's servant, who was very upset that her Queen's son was not being made the crown prince. She poisoned the Queen's mind against this and asked her to invoke the two boons that Dasharatha had granted to her long back – first, to make her son Bharatha, the Crown Prince, and second, to banish Rama from the kingdom for 14 years. Kaikeyi, who was initially very happy to hear the news, slowly was poisoned by Manthara's words that she would lose her position if Rama was crowned and slowly fell into the pit Manthara had dug. She followed Manthara's words and invoked the two boons when Dasharatha came to meet her. The King was heartbroken when he heard these words from Kaikeyi and swooned. He begged Kaikeyi to ask for anything but this, but she did not relent.

Vanavaas – a Journey into the Forests

On hearing this, Rama immediately told his father that he would be away from the kingdom for 14 years to keep up his father's word. He left the palace with his wife, Sita, and his brother, Lakshmana, all clad in saffron robes. These incidents happened in the absence of Bharatha, who had gone to his maternal grandfather's kingdom. When he returned, he was aghast at his mother's actions and refused to accept the throne. Bharatha went to the forest to persuade Rama to return to Ayodhya. When Rama was intent on fulfilling their father's boons to Kaikeyi, Bharatha said he would then rule the kingdom on behalf of his brother Rama until he returned to Ayodhya.

Rama, Sita and Lakshmana travelled long and far by foot and dwelt in small cottages. However, their simple and happy life did not last long. Shoorpanaka, the Lankan princess and sister of Ravana, was offended when neither Rama nor Lakshmana agreed to marry her as per her wishes. She tried to harm Sita, thinking that Rama would marry her if not for Sita. Seeing this, the enraged Lakshmana attacked her, cutting off her nose and ears. She took this to her brother Khara, who grew furious and wanted to avenge this insult. He set out to fight against Rama along with fourteen thousand rakshashas. However, Rama defeated them single-handedly. Soon after, Ravana heard the news of the death of his brothers at the hands of Rama. He took the help of the demon Maricha, who transformed himself into a stunning deer and frolicked around Sita. Sita requested Rama to catch the deer for her. Lakshmana sensed something was amiss and informed his brother that this could be a trick. However, due to Sita's persistent request, Rama followed the deer to capture it, after commanding Lakshmana to protect Sita in the meanwhile. Soon after, Rama slayed the demon Maricha. But as he was dying, he mimicked Rama's voice and called out Lakshmana's name and Sita's name. Hearing the cries, Sita was overcome with fear and coerced Lakshmana to go to Rama's rescue. Making use of this moment, Ravana approached Sita disguised as a Sage and kidnapped her.

The search that followed for Sita was long and hard. Rama happened to meet the Monkey King - Sugriva, who pledged to help Rama with his monkey army. Hanuman - one of them, was the biggest pillar for Rama, who with his utmost devotion towards Rama, travelled to Lanka and found Sita.

Having located Sita, Rama led his monkey army against the Lankan king, Ravana, and vanquished him. He rescued Sita and travelled to Ayodhya in the Pushpaka Vimana, where his subjects welcomed him with great fanfare. Lord Rama was finally crowned the King of Ayodhya!

The Story of Lord Rama was written down by Sage Valmiki to be one of the two Epics of Hinduism, The Ramayana.

The return of Rama, Sita, & Lakshmana to Ayodhya is believed to be celebrated as Diwali in many parts of the country.

Rama Sloka:

Anrsamsyamanukrosah Srutam Silam Damah Samah
Raghavam Sobhayantyete Sadgunah Purusottamam!

Meaning:

Non-violence, compassion, learning, truthful nature, self-control

and tranquillity – these six virtues adorn Rama, the best of men.

EKALAVYA – THE TRUE SPIRIT OF GURU BHAKTHI

Ekalavya was born to Hiranyadhanus, a tribal chief near Hastinapura. Even as a little boy, Ekalavya was interested in learning the nuances of archery and was determined to become a great warrior.

On His Search for Education

He heard about the great Guru, Dronacharya, and travelled to Hastinapura to enrol himself as Drona's student. Drona was then the Royal Guru of the Princes of Hastinapura (The Pandavas & Kauravas). Enquiring about his whereabouts, Drona realised that Ekalavya could not be inducted into the Gurukul (Teacher's place where the students stayed and underwent the education process) where he was supposed to tutor only royal blood. With a heavy heart in turning down a student, Drona sent him away from the Gurukul.

However, Ekalavya, as determined as he was, returned to the forest and sculpted a statue of Dronacharya. He decided that he would practise archery under the supervision of the sculpture of Drona and would consider the sculpture as his Guru. With rigorous practice, Ekalavya soon became an ace archer.

Rendezvous with the Princes

Once, as he was practising his skills, Ekalavya was disturbed by the barking of a dog from a distant place. To silence the continuously barking dog, he used his skills of archery and shot seven consecutive arrows that filled the dog's mouth before the dog could shut its mouth. Just around that moment, the Pandava & Kaurava princes were out on a hunting spree. They spotted the dog with the seven arrows, traced the shooter of the arrows, and found Ekalavya. On enquiring how he acquired such skills of shooting, they were told that Drona was his Guru.

A baffled group of princes left for Hastinapura and immediately approached Drona. Prince Arjuna, the Guru's favourite student, questioned the Guru as to why there was an archer superior to Arjuna himself, when Drona had assured Arjuna earlier that none of his pupils would be equal to Arjuna. On hearing the events of the day, the Guru himself was confused as he had not accepted any other pupil apart from the princes and asked the princes to lead him to the tribal lad.

The Guru Dakshina

Drona had promised Arjuna that he would not let anyone surpass Arjuna in his skills as a warrior, but after seeing Ekalavya, Drona realised that he had not protected his vow. He quickly demanded Guru Dakshina (fee given to teachers for the learning bestowed on students) from Ekalavya.

Ekalavya was only too happy that his Guru had accepted him as his student and was demanding Guru Dakshina. He said he would be ready to give whatever his Guru demanded.

Drona demanded that Ekalavya sever his right thumb and offer it to him as Guru Dakshina. Drona had used this opportunity to make sure his promise did not go in vain. If Ekalavya was disabled, Arjuna would regain his position as the best archer. Without any hesitation, Ekalavya took out his knife and cut his thumb. He offered the same to his Guru, who stood rooted to the spot at the devotion that Ekalavya was exhibiting. He blessed Ekalavya with longstanding fame and left the forest.

Death of Ekalavya

Ekalavya continued practising his archery skills and even without his thumb, rose to become one of the greatest archers of his time. Ekalavya was slain by Lord Krishna in a battle. Lord Krishna explains to Arjuna in the Mahabharata that he had to slay Ekalavya because, if not, Ekalavya would have adopted the side of the Kauravas during the Mahabharata war, making it difficult for the Pandavas to win.

Lord Balarama – The Eighth Avatar

Birth of Balarama

Kamsa, the King of Mathura, had imprisoned his sister Devaki and brother-in-law Vasudeva, since he was warned that the eighth child of the couple would kill him. Even though it was just the eighth child, evil Kamsa had killed the first six children that Devaki gave birth to in the prison. The seventh child that was formed in Devaki's womb was none other than Balarama - but since Lord Vishnu was aware that Kamsa would not let the baby live, he instructed his divine power, Yogamaya, to transfer the child from her womb to Rohini's womb (Rohini was another wife of Vasudeva). Balarama also came to be known as 'Shankarshana'.

Later, Krishna was born as the eighth child and was clandestinely moved to Gokulam, where he grew up as the dear son of Yashoda and Nandagopa.

The Brothers

Balarama and Krishna grew up as half-brothers initially in Gokulam and later in Vrindavan. Balarama was not only Krishna's brother but also his best friend. He won over Asuras like Pralamba and Dhenuka.

During the later parts of his life, he also taught the art of mace fighting to the rival cousins, Bheema and Duryodhana. During the Kurukshetra war, Duryodhana requested Balarama to fight for his cause. However, since Krishna had already taken the Pandavas' side, Balarama refused to fight on the side of the Kauravas as that would amount to fighting against Lord Krishna.

Balarama is also considered a form of the Divine Serpent, Adiseshan, by some sects.

Balarama Sloka:

Goloka-dhamadhipatih pareshvarah
Pareshu mam patu pavitra-kirtanah bhu-mandalam
sarshapavad vilakshyate
Yan-murdhni mam patu sa bhumi-mandale.

Meaning:

Lord Balarama, the Master of Goloka, the supreme controller of all controllers, and whose fame is spotless, please protect me.

May Lord Balarama, who on His head holds the earth as if it were a single mustard seed, protect me in this world.

•••

AANDAAL

Aandaal is one of the twelve Alwar Saints worshipped by the Vaishnavas.

Vishnuchittar, one of the twelve Alwars - also famously known as 'Periyazhwar' - was a devout Brahmin who lived in a small town - Srivilliputhur in Tamil Nadu. He was a staunch devotee of Lord Vishnu and worked in the temple premises to procure flowers for the worship of the Lord.

Kodhai

One day, he found a little baby girl near a Tulasi plant. Having no child of his own, he decided to adopt the little one and named her 'Kodhai'.

Kodhai grew up as a little girl listening to devotional songs and stories about Lord Vishnu and his Avatars, including that of Lord Krishna. She grew fond of Krishna and slowly started imagining herself as His bride.

Every day, without her father's knowledge, she would adorn herself with the flowers and garlands that her father procured for the Lord and replace them in the flower basket. Vishnuchittar, oblivious to these doings, would take the flowers to the temple and adorn the Lord with them. One day, he was surprised and shocked to see a strand of hair in the garland - which he immediately recognised to be Kodhai's. He scolded Kodhai for her unacceptable behaviour of offering to the Lord what was used by her. That night, the Lord appeared in Vishnuchittar's dreams and said he missed the flowers adorned by Kodhai. Much to Vishnuchittar's surprise, the Lord requested Vishnuchittar to offer him the garland which was worn by Kodhai every day.

Vishnuchittar realised the deep love and devotion that Kodhai had for the Lord. Since then, Kodhai came to be known as 'Aandaal', which translates to 'She who ruled', meaning the 'One who ruled over the Lord'.

Aandaal's Wedding!

Once Aandaal reached marriageable age, her father wanted to seek a suitable alliance for her. But she was firm in her decision of marrying Lord Vishnu himself. Vishnuchittar was unaware of how he could fulfil this wish. However, Lord Ranganatha appeared in his dreams and told Vishnuchittar to adorn his daughter as a bride and await his arrival.

On the designated day, Vishnuchittar took his daughter on a palanquin to Srirangam.

Aandaal neared the Sannidhi and became one with the Lord once and for all!

Aandaal was the only female Alwar saint of the twelve Alwars. She is also believed to be an incarnation of Goddess Bhooma Devi.

The day she was found near the Thulasi plant is celebrated as her birth anniversary every year, which falls on the Poora Nakshatra day in the Tamil month of Aadi.

ENCHANTING KRISHNA –
THE NINTH AVATAR

Lord Krishna, the Ninth Avatar of Lord Vishnu, is synonymous with beauty and love. The Hindu scriptures would be incomplete without a mention of this Avatar of Lord Vishnu, since The Bhagavad Gita, one of the holy books of the Hindus, was given to us by Lord Krishna.

The Birth of Krishna

Ugrasena, the king of Mathura, had a brother named Devaka. Ugrasena had a son named Kamsa, and Devaka was blessed with a daughter named Devaki. From his childhood, Kamsa had an inherent affection towards Devaki, his beloved younger sister.

When Devaki got married to Vasudeva, Kamsa was almost in tears, for his beloved sister was leaving them and moving to her in-laws' place. He volunteered to ride the chariot and drive them home, even though he was the crown prince of the state. As he drove away from Mathura, a celestial voice from above called out to Kamsa and exclaimed that the eighth child born of Devaki & Vasudeva would kill him.

The enraged Kamsa got down from his chariot and dragged Devaki onto the ground. He drew his sword out to kill her.

Vasudeva fell at Kamsa's feet and begged him to leave them alone. Kamsa did not relent on any amount of cajoling, and in a bid to save his wife's life, Vasudeva made a promise to Kamsa that he would hand over all the children that his wife gave birth to. Sensing that this would serve the purpose of saving his own life, Kamsa agreed to leave Devaki free.

A year passed, and Devaki gave birth to their first child. Though a joyous occasion, Vasudeva & Devaki were filled with grief since they knew they had to keep up their word and hand over their child to Kamsa. With a heavy heart, Vasudeva carried his child to Kamsa. Surprised at Vasudeva's commitment to keep his word, Kamsa thought to himself that it was only the eighth child that was going to kill him. He thought he could afford to leave the first seven children alive since Vasudeva was also true to his word. He sent back Vasudeva with his child, saying it was enough if he brought the eighth child to him. Overjoyed by the rebirth his child had obtained, Vasudeva returned to his wife with the child. But their joy was not to last for long.

Narada, the divine sage, wanted Lord Krishna to take birth sooner rather than later, for the greater good of the world. He instilled fear in Kamsa's mind that any of Devaki's children could cause him harm. Kamsa, not wanting to take any chances with his life, immediately rode to Devaki's place and demanded that their child be given to him. Though Devaki and Vasudeva resisted his demand, he snatched the child away and killed him. Kamsa also went to the extent of ordering his sister and brother-in-law to be chained in a prison cell so that he could catch hold of each child she delivered.

Years passed, and each time a child was born, Kamsa would be notified by the prison guards. He would snatch the baby from its parents and kill it immediately. Six such children were killed by the wicked Kamsa. The seventh child in Devaki's womb was a part-manifestation of Lord Vishnu. Lord Vishnu ordered Yogamaya to transfer the child from Devaki's womb to Rohini's womb (Rohini was another wife of Vasudeva, who lived in Gokulam). This child then grew up to be Balarama.

Birth of Krishna

The eighth child was none other than Lord Vishnu who had taken his Avatar as Lord Krishna to vanquish all evil on earth. On the night of his birth, the skies thundered, and there was a heavy downpour of rain. As soon as the child was born, a voice was heard from the Lord Himself, instructing Vasudeva to secretly take the baby to Gokulam and leave him in the house of Nandagopa, the chief of the Yadava clan in Gokulam. He also instructed Vasudeva to bring back the baby that was born in Nandagopa's house around the same time. As advised, Vasudeva escaped from the prison cell and carried the baby in a basket to Gokulam. The rains lashed, and Sesha, the serpent, came over to give protection to the divine baby. Soon after Vasudeva reached Gokulam, he headed towards Nandagopa's house and laid the baby beside

Yashodha, Nandagopa's wife, who had just delivered a baby girl. Vasudeva returned to the prison carrying the baby girl and placed it near Devaki.

As soon as Kamsa was notified that Devaki had given birth to her eighth child, he hurried to the prison cell. As he seized the baby girl by her feet to kill her, she slipped from his hand and rose up in the air. The baby girl stood incarnated as Goddess Durga. She had taken birth as Yogamaya, the baby girl born to Yashodha and Nandagopa. She proclaimed, "Your enemy is already safe in another house! It is no use trying to kill me!" Saying this, she vanished into thin air. Kamsa was determined to catch hold of the baby and kill him as soon as possible to save his own life. But far from all this commotion, little baby Krishna lay deeply asleep, safe and sound. The Hindu tradition celebrates his birthday as 'Gokulashtami' or 'Janmashtami'.

Krishna's Childhood

Krishna grew up in Gokulam for a few years and then moved to Vrindavan. He lived the life of a cowherd along with his brother, Balarama, and his other friends. Krishna is known to have performed most of his Krishnaleelas at this place. Kalinga Narthana, lifting the Govardhan hill to protect the inmates of Vrindavan, and getting rid of demons like Bakasura and Agasura who were sent by Kamsa to kill Krishna were some of the leelas by him. Once, Krishna and Balarama visited Mathura and killed Mushtika & Chanura, champion wrestlers. In the ensuing face-off with Kamsa, he killed Kamsa and ended the demon's tyranny on the people of Mathura. He then crowned his grandfather, Ugrasena, as the King of Mathura.

Krishna in the Mahabharata

Krishna played an important role in the epic Mahabharata by negotiating between the Pandavas and Kauravas in a very turbulent environment. However, when his attempts at reasoning with Duryodhana failed, he stood by the Pandavas to protect Dharma. When Arjuna felt low during the Battle of Kurukshetra, Lord Krishna delivered The Bhagavad Gita – a divine and spiritual message that provides us with the right guidance towards moral living and self-realisation.

From being a mischievous little baby, a charming boy, a mesmerising lover, to being a protector of Dharma, he never failed to enchant us in any of his facets. He truly remains the Enchanting Lord!

Krishna Sloka:

Vasudeva Sutam Devam, Kamsa Chaanuuramardanam
Devaki Paramaanandam Krishnam, Vande Jagad Gurum

Meaning:

Krishna, the Supreme Lord, the Son of Devaki and Vasudeva, the slayer of Kamsa and Chanur. May we bow to Him and be blessed with the God's grace.